Chinese
Stories
Book 3

for Beginners with Pinyin, English and Audio

Hong Meng 鴻蒙

Table of Contents

Introduction

This book is perfect for beginners who want to enhance their reading skills. There are 20 simple and easy to read short stories for absolute beginners who just started to learn Chinese. This is the 3rd book in the Chinese Stories Series.

The Chinese language has 4 tones and a silent tone and it consists of hundreds of thousands of words. Therefore, a better way to learn Chinese is to read and listen more.

The Pinyin is placed on top of the Chinese characters. Together with our audio files, you will be able to speed up your learning in an enjoyable way.

There are many Chinese idioms used in the stories. This will enhance your understanding on how and when the idioms are used.

The link and password to **download all the audio files** is at the end of the book.

Chinese Stories for Beginners Series

【1】上网的小老鼠

老鼠 一 家 开开心心 地 生活 在
山洞 里。 有 一 天，爸爸 到 大 城市
出差，带回 来 一 台 笔记本电脑。 没
想到，这 台 笔记本电脑 把 小 老鼠 给
吸引 住了。它 每天 从 早 玩 到 晚，不
是 上网 浏览 网页，就是 玩 网络 游戏，
上了 瘾。 老鼠 妈妈 和 老鼠 爸爸 多次
制止，小 老鼠 都 不 听。 小 老鼠 每次 都
趁 它们 上班 地 时候 偷偷 玩 电脑，
眼睛 看 得 通红 。

一 天，老鼠 爸爸 和 老鼠 妈妈 想
到了 一个 好 注意，它们 把 电脑 藏了 起来，

并 对 小 老鼠 说："孩子，爸爸 妈妈 已经 把 电脑 锁起来 了，今后 不许 玩 电脑 了！" 说完 便 离开 了。它们 走 后，小 老鼠 到处 找 电脑，终于 在 床 底下 找到了。他 开开心心 的 打开 电脑，正要 拿 鼠标 玩 游戏，忽然 一 只 大花 猫 出现 在 它 眼前，对着 它 "喵 喵" 直 叫。小 老鼠 吓坏 了，抱头鼠窜 。

躲 在一 旁 的 老鼠 爸爸 和 老鼠 妈妈 偷偷 地 笑了。原来 它们 把 小 老鼠 的 游戏 换成 了 "花 猫 写真"。

从此，小 老鼠 再 也 不敢 玩 电脑了，因为 它 怕 点 开 哪个 图标，在 跳出 一只 花 猫 来。

[1] Little Mouse on the Internet
English Translation

老鼠一家开开心心地生活在山洞里。有一天，爸爸到大城市出差，带回来一台笔记本电脑。没想到，这台笔记本电脑把小老鼠给吸引住了。它每天从早玩到晚，不是上网浏览网页，就是玩网络游戏，上了瘾。老鼠妈妈和老鼠爸爸多次制止，小老鼠都不听。小老鼠每次都趁它们上班地时候偷偷玩电脑，眼睛看得通红。

The mouse family lived happily in the cave. One day, Dad went to the big city on business and brought back a laptop computer. Didn't expect the little mouse to be addicted to playing it. Each day, the little mouse will either browse the Internet or play online games. The mouse mother and the mouse father tried to stop the little mouse many times, but the little mouse wouldn't listen to them. Every time after they go to work, the little mouse secretly use the laptop.

一天，老鼠爸爸和老鼠妈妈想到了一个好注意，它们把电脑藏了起来，并对小老鼠说："孩子，爸爸妈妈已经把电脑锁起来了，今后不许玩电脑了！"说完便离开了。它们走后，小老鼠到处找电脑，终于在床底下找到了。他开开心心的打开电脑，正要拿鼠标玩游戏，忽然一只大花猫出现在它眼前，对着它"喵喵"直叫。小老鼠吓坏了，抱头鼠窜。

One day, mouse father and mouse mother thought of a good idea, they hid the laptop, and said to the little mouse: "Child, mom and dad have locked up the laptop, from now on you are not allowed to play the laptop!" After that, its parents left. After they left, the little mouse went to look for the laptop and finally found it under the bed. He happily switched on the laptop, and when the little mouse is about to play a computer game, suddenly a big cat appeared in front of it. The little mouse was so frightened.

躲在一旁的老鼠爸爸和老鼠妈妈偷偷地笑了。原来它们把小老鼠的游戏换成了"花猫写真"。

The mouse father and the mother mouse were hiding on the side, secretly watching the little mouse. It turned out that they had replaced the game with "real cat" game.

从此，小老鼠再也不敢玩电脑了，因为它怕点开哪个图标，在跳出一只花猫来。

From then on, the little mouse no longer dares to play with the laptop, because it is afraid that a cat would jump out.

【2】我的汉语老师

Wǒ de Hànyǔ lǎoshī xìng bái tā dàizhe yí fù
我 的 汉语 老师 姓 白,他 戴着 一 副
jīnsī biān yǎnjìng tóufa zhǎngcháng de hěn piàoliang
金丝 边 眼镜,头发 长长 的,很 漂亮 。

Bái lǎoshī jiāo wǒmen yǔwén tā jiǎngkè
白 老师 教 我们 语文 ,他 讲课
shēngdòng shēngyīn qīngcuì wǒmen chángcháng bèi
生动 , 声音 清脆,我们 常常 被
tā de kè xīyǐn Zài kètáng shàng bái lǎoshī búdàn
她 的 课 吸引。 在 课堂 上 ,白 老师 不但
jiāo gěi wǒmen zhīshi hái jiāo wǒmen zěnmeyàng zuòrén
教 给 我们 知识,还 教 我们 怎么样 做人,
gǔlì wǒmen nǔlì xuéxí cóngxiǎo dǎhǎo jīchǔ
鼓励 我们 努力 学习, 从小 打好 基础,
jiānglái yíngjiē shèhuì de tiǎozhàn Lìngwài zài kètáng
将来 迎接 社会 的 挑战 。 另外,在 课堂
shàng tā hái chángcháng hé wǒmen yìqǐ chànggē
上 她 还 常常 和 我们 一起 唱歌,
tiàowǔ ne
跳舞 呢!

Bái lǎoshī zǒngshì miàndài xiàoróng shuōhuà
白 老师 总是 面带 笑容 , 说话

温和 可亲。 同学们 都 爱 依偎 在 她
身边，和 她 聊天，听 她 讲 动人 的 故事。
我们 都 很 喜欢 她。

[2] My Chinese Teacher
English Translation

我的汉语老师姓白，他戴着一副金丝边眼镜，头发长长的，很漂亮。

My Chinese teacher's last name is Bai, she wears a pair of gold-frame glasses, has long hair, very beautiful.

白老师教我们语文，他讲课生动，声音清脆，我们常常被她的课吸引。在课堂上，白老师不但教给我们知识，还教我们怎么样做人，鼓励我们努力学习，从小打好基础，将来迎接社会的挑战。另外，在课堂上她还常常和我们一起唱歌，跳舞呢!

Teacher Bai teaches us the Chinese language. Her lectures are vivid, and her voice is crisp. We are often attracted to her classes. In the classroom, Teacher Bai not only teaches us knowledge but also teaches us how to be a good person, encourages us to study hard, to lay a good foundation from an early age, that meet the challenges of a society in the future. She also often sang and danced with us in class!

白老师总是面带笑容，说话温和可亲。同学们都爱依偎在她身边，和她聊天，听她讲动人的故事。我们都很喜欢她。

Teacher Bai always has a smile on her face and a soft-spoken voice. The students loved to snuggle around her, chat with her, and listen to her telling touching stories. We all like her very much.

【3】一本有趣的书

Yì tiān bàngwǎn yì jiārén zhǔnbèi chī wǎnfàn
一 天　傍晚，一 家人　准备　吃　晚饭

le bàba gāngyào dòng kuàizi què bèi māma lánzhu le
了,爸爸　刚要　动　筷子,却　被　妈妈　拦住　了:

Érzi dào nǎr qù le Kuài qù jiào érzi chīfàn
"儿子 到 哪儿 去 了? 快 去 叫 儿子 吃饭!"

Tīngle māma de huà bàba biàn zhǐhǎo qù
听了　妈妈　的　话,爸爸　便　只好　去

shūfáng jiào érzi lái chīfàn Bàba yì tuī kāimén jiù
书房　叫 儿子 来 吃饭。 爸爸 一 推　开门,就

tīngjiàn érzi xīxi-hāhā dì xiào ge bùtíng
听见　儿子 "嘻嘻哈哈" 地　笑　个　不停。。。

Bàba hǎndào Érzi kuài chīfàn le Biékàn le Érzi
爸爸　喊道:"儿子 快 吃饭 了! 别看 了!" 儿子

tīng le què shěbude líkāi Kěshì bàba yízài dūncù
听 了,却 舍不得 离开。 可是 爸爸 一再 敦促,

érzi zhǐhǎo guāiguāi dechū qù le Bàba jiàn érzi
儿子 只好　乖乖　地出　去 了。 爸爸 见 儿子

zǒu le piǎole yìyǎn shū
走 了,瞟了 一眼 书。。。

儿子 来到 餐桌 后，却 发现 爸爸 不见 了，妈妈 问："爸爸 呢?" 儿子 只好 去书房 找 爸爸，看见 爸爸 正 躺 在地上 看 自己 刚才 看 的 书 呢! 他 立刻 对爸爸 大声 喊道："爸爸，吃饭 了! 别看 书了!"

爸爸 听 了，只好 和 儿子 一起 来到餐桌 旁 老老实实 地 吃 起 饭 来。

[3] An Interesting Book
English Translation

一天傍晚，一家人准备吃晚饭了，爸爸刚要动筷子，却被妈妈拦住了："儿子到哪儿去了？快去叫儿子吃饭！"

One evening, a family was ready for dinner, as soon as the father picked up the chopsticks, the mother stopped him and asked: "Where's our son?" Go and get our son to dinner! "

听了妈妈的话，爸爸便只好去书房叫儿子来吃饭。爸爸一推开门，就听见儿子"嘻嘻哈哈"地笑个不停。。。爸爸喊道："儿子快吃饭了！别看了！"儿子听了，却舍不得离开。可是爸爸一再敦促，儿子只好乖乖地出去了。爸爸见儿子走了，瞟了一眼书。。。

After hearing that, the father had to go to the study room to look for the son. As soon as the father pushed the door open, he listened to his son laughing non-stop... so the father shouted, "Son, go and eat! Don't read anymore!" The son heard his father but was reluctant to leave. But the father repeatedly urged that the son to have dinner. After the son left, the father glanced at the book...

　　儿子来到餐桌后，却发现爸爸不见了，妈妈问："爸爸呢？"儿子只好去书房找爸爸，看见爸爸正躺在地上看自己刚才看的书呢！他立刻对爸爸大声喊道："爸爸，吃饭了！别看书了！"

　　When the son came to the table, the father was nowhere to be seen, and the mother asked, "Where's your father?" The son had no choice but to go to the study room to look for his father. He found his father lying on the ground reading the book he had just read! He immediately shouted at his father, "Dad, eat! Don't read anymore!"

　　爸爸听了，只好和儿子一起来到餐桌旁老老实实地吃起饭来。

　　After the father heard the son, he had no choice but to go to the dining table with his son to have dinner.

【4】太婆的嘴角

Jīntiān shì tàipó bāshí dàshòu jiā lǐ de qīnqi
今天 是 太婆 八十 大寿，家 里 的 亲戚
dōu gǎnlái wèi tàipó zhùshòu
都 赶来 为 太婆 祝寿 。

Shūshu yì jiā lái le gūgu yì jiā yě lái le
叔叔 一 家 来 了，姑姑 一 家 也 来 了，
jiā lǐ dàochù dōu shì rén dàochù dōu chōngmǎnle
家 里 到处 都 是 人，到处 都 充满了
huānshēng-xiàoyǔ Tàipó dōu lè kāile huā zuǐjiǎo
欢声笑语 。 太婆 都 乐 开了 花，嘴角
yìzhí shàngyángzhe
一直 上扬着 。

Wǎnfàn hòu dàjiā yígègè dōu huíjiā le rènao
晚饭 后，大家 一个个 都 回家 了，热闹
de xiǎo yuàn yíxià lěngqīngle qǐlai Wǒ kànjiàn
的 小 院 一下 冷清了 起来。 我 看见
tàipó yí ge rén zuò zài jiǎoluò mīfeng zhuóyǎn
太婆 一个 人 坐 在 角落，眯缝 着眼，
xiàoróng bú jiàn le
笑容 不见 了。

我 走过 去，挨着 太婆 坐着，不 知道 该 说 些 什么。

唉，要是 大家 在 平时 也 能 多 回来 看看 太婆，那 太婆 的 嘴角 肯定 就 会 一直 上扬着 吧！

[4] My Great Grandmother
English Translation

今天是太婆八十大寿，家里的亲戚都赶来为太婆祝寿。

Today is the 80th birthday of my great grandmother, all the family's relatives are coming to celebrate her birthday.

叔叔一家来了，姑姑一家也来了，家里到处都是人，到处都充满了欢声笑语。太婆都乐开了花，嘴角一直上扬着。

Uncle's family came, aunt's family also came, the house is full of people, everywhere is filled with laughter. My great grandmother was so happy that the corners of her mouth were always wide open.

晚饭后，大家一个个都回家了，热闹的小院一下冷清了起来。我看见太婆一个人坐在角落，眯缝着眼，笑容不见了。

After dinner, everyone went home one by one, and the lively courtyard was deserted. I saw great grandmother sitting alone in the corner, squinting and her smiles disappeared.

　　我走过去，挨着太婆坐着，不知道该说些什么。

　　I walked over to sit with her, not knowing what to say to her.

　　唉，要是大家在平时也能多回来看看太婆，那太婆的嘴角肯定就会一直上扬着吧！

　　Hey, if everyone can come back to see the great grandmother all the time, the corner of her mouth will definitely go up!

【5】胆小的我

Wǒ de dǎnzi tèbié xiǎo xiǎo dé xiàng zhǐ xiǎo
我 的 胆子 特别 小，小 得 像 只 小
báitù
白兔。

Jìde yǒu yì tiān wǎnshang wǒ yǐjing tǎng zài
记得 有 一 天 晚上，我 已经 躺 在
chuángshàng le yòu tūrán xiǎng hēshuǐ kě sìzhōu tài
床上 了，又 突然 想 喝水，可 四周 太
hēi le zěnme yě bùgǎn xiàchuáng Yǒule Wǒ
黑 了，怎么 也 不敢 下床 。 有了！我
shùnshǒu náqǐ shǒudiàntǒng Wǒ xiàle chuáng
顺手 拿起 手电筒 。 我 下了 床，
wǎngqián zǒu suīrán yǒu shǒudiàntǒng zhàozhe liàng
往前 走，虽然 有 手电筒 照着 亮，
bùzěnme hēi dàn hái shì tíxīn-diàodǎn Yuè shì hàipà
不怎么 黑，但 还是 提心吊胆 。 越 是 害怕，
diànshìjù lǐ de guǐ gùshi yuè zài nǎohǎi lǐ chūxiàn wǒ
电视剧 里 的 鬼 故事 越 在 脑海 里 出现，我
bùyóude dǎ qí duōsuo lái Suīrán shǒudiàntǒng
不由得 打 其 哆嗦 来。 虽然 手电筒
zhàozhe yí ge rén wǒ xià dé dàshēng hǎn māma
照着 一个 "人"，我 吓 得 大声 喊 妈妈，
māma guòlai shí wǒ lián dàqì de bùgǎn chū jǐnjǐn de
妈妈 过来 时 我 连 大气 地 不敢 出，紧紧 地

扶住了 墙，妈妈 打 开灯 一 看，原来 是
衣服 架 上 的 一 件 衣服。 这时，我 才
想起来，这 是 傍晚 时我 挂上 去 的
衣服，没 想到 自己 吓了 自己。

晚上 我 总是 把家 里 所有 的 灯
都 打开。 我 真 希望 我 能 变成 一个
胆大 的 人。

[5] The Timid me
English Translation

我的胆子特别小，小得像只小白兔。

My guts are very small, small as a little white rabbit.

记得有一天晚上，我已经躺在床上了，又突然想喝水，可四周太黑了，怎么也不敢下床。有了！我顺手拿起手电筒。我下了床，往前走，虽然有手电筒照着亮，不怎么黑，但还是提心吊胆。越是害怕，电视剧里的鬼故事越在脑海里出现，我不由得打其哆嗦来。虽然手电筒照着一个"人"，我吓得大声喊妈妈，妈妈过来时我连大气地不敢出，紧紧地扶住了墙，妈妈打开灯一看，原来是衣服架上的一件衣服。这时，我才想起来，这是傍晚时我挂上去的衣服，没想到自己吓了自己。

I remember one night when I was lying in bed, suddenly I wanted to drink water, but all around is too dark, I don't dare to get out of bed. Got it! I can use the flashlight. I got out of bed, and although the flashlight shines brightly, not too dark, I am still afraid. The more afraid I am, the more ghost stories in the TV series came to my mind. But I told myself I have to soldier on. The flashlight shines on a "person", I was scared screamed for my mother, when my mother came, I didn't even dare to breathe but held on tightly to the wall. My mother turned on the lamp to see, it was a dress hanging on the clothes' hanger. I suddenly remembered that earlier in the evening, I hung up the clothes there. I am just scaring myself.

晚上我总是把家里所有的灯都打开。我真希望我能变成一个胆大的人。

I always turn on all the lights in my house in the evening. I wish that one day, I could be a bold man.

【6】芭比娃娃

我 的 玩具 很 多, 但 我 最 喜欢 的 事

芭 比 娃娃。 芭 比 娃娃 的 个子 很 高, 披着

长长 的 金发, 脚 上 穿着 一 双

大 红色 的 高跟鞋, 很 好看 。 她 总是

面带 微笑, 非常 招人 喜欢。

她 有 五 套 衣服:一 套 泳衣, 一 套

睡衣, 一 套 粉色 连衣裙, 一 套 紫色 纱 裙, 一

套 黄色 制服。 这 五 套 衣服 可 漂亮 了,

我 早上 给 她 穿上 制服, 代表 她 去

上班 ; 中午 给 她 换上 泳衣, 代表

她 去 游泳;下午 给 她 穿 连衣裙, 代表

她 游泳 结束；晚上 我 给 她 穿上
睡衣，让 她 在 我 的 枕头 边 入睡。

[6] Barbie Doll
English Translation

　　我的玩具很多，但我最喜欢的事芭比娃娃。芭比娃娃的个子很高，披着长长的金发，脚上穿着一双大红色的高跟鞋，很好看。她总是面带微笑，非常招人喜欢。

　　I have a lot of toys, but my favourite thing is Barbie. Barbie is tall, with long blonde hair and a pair of red heels on her feet. She is always smiling and very attractive.

　　她有五套衣服：一套泳衣，一套睡衣，一套粉色连衣裙，一套紫色纱裙，一套黄色制服。这五套衣服可漂亮了，我早上给她穿上制服，代表她去上班；中午给她换上泳衣，代表她去游泳；下午给她穿连衣裙，代表她游泳结束；晚上我给她穿上睡衣，让她在我的枕头边入睡。

　　She has five sets of clothes: a bathing suit, a pyjama, a pink one-piece dress, a purple dress, a yellow uniform. These five sets of clothes are beautiful, I put on her uniform in the morning to represent that she is going to work, change into her bathing suit at noon so that she can go for a swim, dress her in the afternoon, represents that she has finished her swim. In the evening, I put her in her pyjamas and put her to sleep by my pillow.

【7】花园见闻

一个 周末，我 去 我 家 旁边 的
花园 里 玩。 花园 里面 的 花 开 得 真
鲜艳 啊，似乎 给 花园 涂上了 色彩；花园
里面 的 花 开 得 真 美 啊，仿佛 是 天上
地 仙女 下凡；花园 里的 花 开 得 真 香
啊， 刚刚 走进 花园 就 好像 被 花香
包围 了。

啊， 远处 的 大 哥哥 竟然 摘了 一 朵
花，还有 一 位 大姐姐 也 正 准备 摘花。
唉，他们 不 应该 这么 做 呀。 他们 被
管理员 叔叔 发现 了， 管理员 叔叔

批评了 他们。 看 他们 的 样子，一定 是
认识 到了 自己 的 错误。

他们 怎么 拿着 水桶 回来 了？ 原来，
他们 要 给 美丽 的 花儿 浇水 啊。 他们
笑 得 多 开心 啊。 浇过 水 后 的 花 更
美 了，似乎 在 笑着 说："谢谢 你们，你们
真 是 知 错 就 改 的 好 孩子."

我 该 回家 了。 就 在 我 走到 花园
门口 得 时候，我 听到 身后 传来了
说话 声 。 原来 是 管理员 叔叔 和 大
哥哥，大姐姐 告别 呢。 我 想，他们 以后
一定 不 会 再 摘花 了。

[7] Garden Knowledge
English Translation

一个周末，我去我家旁边的花园里玩。花园里面的花开得真鲜艳啊，似乎给花园涂上了色彩；花园里面的花开得真美啊，仿佛时天上地仙女下凡；花园里的花开得真香啊，刚刚走进花园就好像被花香包围了。

One weekend, I went to play in the garden next to my house. The flowers in the garden are really bright, it seems to paint the entire garden with colours; the flowers in the garden are really beautiful, as if the heavenly fairy came down from the sky; the flowers in the garden are really fragrant, as I walked into the garden I am surrounded by flowers' fragrance.

啊，远处的大哥哥竟然摘了一朵花，还有一位大姐姐也正准备摘花。唉，它们不应该这么做呀。他们被管理员叔叔发现了，管理员叔叔批评了他们。看他们的样子，一定是认识到了自己的错误。

Ah, the big brother in the distance just picked up a flower, and a big sister is also preparing to pick flowers. Alas, they shouldn't have done that. The adminsitrator discovered them picking flowers and criticized them. Looking at them now, they must be aware of their own mistakes.

他们怎么拿着水桶回来了？原来，他们要给美丽的花儿浇水啊。他们笑得多开心啊。浇过水后的花更美了，似乎在笑着说："谢谢你们，你们真是知错就改的好孩子."

Why did they come back with the bucket? It turned out that they were going to water the beautiful flowers. They laughed so happily. After watering the flowers, the flowers became more beautiful, and they seem to be laughing and saying: "Thank you, you know what you have done wrong and changed, you are such good kids."

我该回家了。就在我走到花园门口得时候，我听到身后传来了说话声。原来时管理员叔叔和大哥哥，大姐姐告别呢。我想，他们以后一定不会再摘花了。

It's time for me to go home. Just as I was walking to the garden gate, I heard a voice behind me. It is the administrator uncle, big brother and big sister bidding farewell. I don't think they'll pick up the flowers again.

【8】鞋子和袜子

袜子 羡慕 鞋子 每天 都 可以 呼吸道
新鲜 的 空气,鞋子 也 羡慕 袜子 的 悠闲 。
经过 一番 商量 ,它们 俩 换了 工作 。
鞋子 在 里面,袜子 在 外面 。

小主人 穿着 它们 出去 散步 。
袜子 终于 呼吸 到了 新鲜 的 空气,鞋子 也
感到 舒服 多 了 。 可是 不久,袜子 就 杯
磨破 了, 小主人 光着 叫 感到 硌 得
慌 ,就 把 袜子 和 鞋子 扔 了,又 去 买了 一
双 新 袜子 和 鞋子。

[8] Shoes and Socks
English Translation

袜子羡慕鞋子每天都可以呼吸道新鲜的空气，鞋子也羡慕袜子的悠闲。经过一番商量，它们俩换了工作。鞋子在里面，袜子在外面。

Socks envy shoes because the shoes can breathe fresh air every day. The shoes also envy socks because it is comfortably lying inside. After some discussion, the two of them changed their jobs. The shoes will be inside, and the socks will be outside.

小主人穿着它们出去散步。袜子终于呼吸到了新鲜的空气，鞋子也感到舒服多了。可是不久，袜子就杯磨破了，小主人光着叫感到硌得慌，就把袜子和鞋子扔了，又去买了一双新袜子和鞋子。

The little master wore them out for a walk. The socks finally manage to breathe some fresh air, and the shoes feel much more comfortable being inside. But soon, the socks on the heel wore out, the little master just cried and panicked, so he threw the socks and shoes away, and went to buy a new pair of socks and shoes.

【9】团结的蚂蚁

今天 课间 活动 时,我 看见 许多 蚂蚁 正在 忙碌,它们 很 有秩序 地 爬着, 它们 在 干什么 呢?我 蹲下 身子 仔细 地 观察 起来。

蚂蚁们 好像 在 用 触角 交流,它们 遇见 同伴 就 停下来,用 触角 你 碰 碰 我,我 碰 碰 你,似乎 在 说:"前面 有 个 大 东西,可 好 吃 了!我自己 搬 不动,快 去 叫 些 伙伴 来,大家 一起 搬。"

它们 一只 接着 一只,组 成了 一支 浩浩荡荡 的 长队 。 它们 一边 走,

一边 用 头上 的 触须 碰 一下 对面 走过来 的 蚂蚁。 最后，它们 齐心协力，不一会儿 就 把 食物 搬 进了 家。 我 还 没 反应 过来，它们 就 已经 收工 了。

看着 看着，我 更加 喜欢 这些 黑色 的 小 生灵 了。 它们 告诉 我，集体 的 力量 是 很 强大 的。 一定 要 团结。

[9] Solidarity ants
English Translation

今天课间活动时，我看见许多蚂蚁正在忙碌，它们很有秩序地爬着，它们在干什么呢？我蹲下身子仔细地观察起来。

During today's inter-class activities, I saw a lot of very busy ants climbing orderly, what are they doing? I crouched down and observed them.

蚂蚁们好像在用触角交流，它们遇见同伴就停下来，用触角你碰碰我，我碰碰你，似乎在说："前面有个大东西，可好吃了！我自己搬不动，快去叫些伙伴来，大家一起搬。"

Ants seem to be using their tentacles to communicate with each other, and they stopped to greet the opposite ant with their tentacles, the ant seems to say to the opposite ant: "There is a big thing in front, it can be delicious! I can't move it on my own, please get more ants to come, we'll move it together. "

它们一只接着一只，组成了一支浩浩荡荡的长队。它们一边走，一边用头上的触须碰一下对面走过来的蚂蚁。最后，它们齐心协力，不一会儿就把食物搬进了家。我还没反应过来，它们就已经收工了。

　　They, one after another, formed a vast long line. As they walked, they touched the ants on the opposite side with the tentacles on their heads. In the end, they grouped and moved the food into their house. They're done before I have time to reflect.

　　看着看着，我更加喜欢这些黑色的小生灵了。它们告诉我，集体的力量是很强大的。一定要团结。

　　Looking at them, I like these little black creatures more. They taught me that collective effort is powerful. Must be united.

【10】对岸的桃子树

一天，小猴和小兔相约到外面玩。它们来到小河边，抬头一看，发现对岸有一棵桃子树。树上结满了大大的桃子，使它们直流口水。怎么样才能够吃到桃子呢？它们坐在河边思考着。游过去？可是，它们不会游泳。

小兔伤心地说："如果有船就好了，可是，船在哪里找呢？"

"木头不就可以当船吗？"小猴拍了一下脑袋说道。

这是一个好办法。小猴和小兔连忙跑到旁边的森林里，找来了一根又长又粗的木头。可是，这根木头太重了。"我们一起搬吧。"小兔提议道。

于是，它们搬着这根木头回到了河边。这下子，它们终于来到了河对岸，吃上了那又香又甜的桃子。

"谢谢你，是你让我吃上了桃子。"

"我也要谢谢你帮助我搬这根木头。"

[10] Peach tree on the Opposite Bank
English Translation

一天，小猴和小兔相约到外面玩。它们来到小河边，抬头一看，发现对岸有一棵桃子树。树上结满了大大的桃子，使它们直流口水。怎么样才能够吃到桃子呢？它们坐在河边思考着。游过去？可是，它们不会游泳。

One day, the monkey and the rabbit met to play outside. They came to the river, looked up and saw a peach tree on the opposite bank. The trees were covered with large peaches, making them drool instantly. How can they eat peaches? They sat by the river thinking. Swim over? However, they can't swim.

小兔伤心地说："如果有船就好了，可是，船在哪里找呢？"

Rabbit said sadly: "If only there is a boat, but, where can we find a boat?"

"木头不就可以当船吗？"小猴拍了一下脑袋说道。

"Can't we use wood as a boat?" The little monkey patted his head and said.

这是一个好办法。小猴和小兔连忙跑到旁边的森林里，找来了一根又长又粗的木头。可是，这根木头太重了。"我们一起扛吧。"小兔提议道。

This is a good idea. The little monkey and the rabbit hurriedly ran to the nearby forest and found a long, thick piece of wood. But the wood was too heavy. "Let's carry it together." Rabbit suggested.

于是，它们扛着这根木头回到了河边。这下子，它们终于来到了河对岸，吃上了那又香又甜的桃子。

So they carried the wood back to the river. This time, they finally reached the other side of the river, and get to eat those fragrant and sweet peaches.

"谢谢你，是你让我吃上了桃子。"

"Thank you, because of you I get to eat these peaches."

"我也要谢谢你帮助我扛这根木头。"

"I would also like to thank you for helping me carry this wood. "

【11】雨伞该给谁

一天，青蛙，乌龟，鸭子和大公鸡准备到好朋友小山羊的家里去做客。忽然，天上飘来了一片乌云，很快就下起了大雨，小动物们只能冒雨赶路。

当小动物们经过小花猫家时，小花猫正好看见它们在冒雨赶路，连忙进屋拿了一把雨伞。可是，这把雨伞该给谁呢？小花猫心里想：青蛙，乌龟，鸭子一定不怕雨，因为它们经常在水里玩儿，所以这把雨伞应该

给 大 公鸡。 于是，小花 猫 赶紧 把 雨伞
给了 大 公鸡,大 公鸡 很 感动 。

就 这样， 小动物 们 顺利 地 到达了
小 山羊 的 家。

[11] Umbrella for Who?
English Translation

　　一天，青蛙，乌龟，鸭子和大公鸡准备到好朋友小山羊的家里去做客。忽然，天上飘来了一片乌云，很快就下起了大雨，小动物们只能冒雨赶路。

　　One day, frog, turtle, duck and big rooster were getting ready to visit their good friend, little goat. Suddenly, a dark cloud floated in the sky, and soon it rained heavily, and the animals had to rush through the rain to continue their journey.

　　当小动物们经过小花猫家时，小花猫正好看见它们在冒雨赶路，连忙进屋拿了一把雨伞。可是，这把雨伞该给谁呢？小花猫心里想：青蛙，乌龟，鸭子一定不怕雨，因为它们经常在水里玩儿，所以这把雨伞应该给大公鸡。于是，小花猫赶紧把雨伞给了大公鸡，大公鸡很感动。

　　When the little animals passed the cat's house, the cat saw them rushing through the rain, and the cat hurried into its house to take an umbrella. But who should this umbrella be given to? The cat thought: frog, turtle, duck are not afraid of rain, because they often play in the water, so this umbrella should be given to the big rooster. The cat hastened to give the umbrella to the big rooster. The big was very touched.

就这样，小动物们顺利地到达了小山羊的家。

In this way, the little animals successfully reached the little goat's house.

【12】学煮牛奶

今天，妈妈 不 在家，我 便 自己 学着 煮 牛奶。

我 先 拿起 剪刀 剪开 牛奶 袋，把 牛奶 倒进 锅 里，接着 把 锅 放到 炉子 上 。"啪"，我 打开了 按钮，缺点 不着 煤气。 咦？奇怪，怎么 点 不 着火 呀？没 火，这 牛奶 怎么 煮 呢？哦！原来 是 我 忘了 开 煤气 阀门 了，哈哈！

煮了 一会儿，我 忽然 听到 "哗" 的 一 声响 ，于是 我 赶紧 转身 去 看，呀， 牛奶 从 锅 里 溢出 来 了！吓 得 我 急忙

关了 煤气 阀门。 幸好 我 关 火 及时，才
保住了 半 瓶 奶。

真 没 想到，煮 牛奶 也 是 一 件 挺
难 的 事。

[12] Learn How to Boil Milk
English Translation

今天，妈妈不在家，我便自己学着煮牛奶。

Today, my mother is not at home, and I learned to boil milk by myself.

我先拿起剪刀剪开牛奶袋，把牛奶倒进锅里，接着把锅放到炉子上。"啪"，我打开了按钮，缺点不着煤气。咦？奇怪，怎么点不着火呀？没火，这牛奶怎么煮呢？哦！原来是我忘了开煤气阀门了，哈哈！

I first picked up the scissors to cut the milk bag, poured the milk into the pot, and then put the pot on the stove. "Pop", I turned the gas on, but there is no gas. Hey? Strange, why can't I light the stove? No fire, how can I boil the milk? Oh! It turned out that I forgot to turn the gas valve, haha!

煮了一会儿，我忽然听到"哗"的一声响，于是我赶紧转身去看，呀，牛奶从锅里溢出来了！吓得我急忙关了煤气阀门。幸好我关火及时，才保住了半瓶奶。

After cooking for a while, I suddenly heard a sound, so I quickly turned around to see, ah, milk overflowed from the pot! I was so frightened that I shut down the gas valve in a hurry. Fortunately, I shut down the fire in time, and I could save half a bottle of milk.

真没想到，煮牛奶也是一件挺难的事。

I didn't expect that cooking milk can be a tough thing to do.

【13】 商量

Jīntiān wǒ hé jiějie yìqǐ zài tā jiā lǐ wán
今天，我 和 姐姐 一起 在 她 家 里 玩。

Wánzhe wánzhe tā xiǎng qù wàimian wán kě wǒ què
玩着 玩着，她 想 去 外面 玩，可 我 却

xiǎng qù wǒ jiā wán
想 去 我 家 玩。

Zhè kě zěnme bàn ne Wǒliǎ shāngliangle
这 可 怎么 办 呢？我俩 商量了

bàntiān dōu jiānchí zìjǐ de yìjian Zhèshí wǒmen
半天，都 坚持 自己 的 意见。 这时，我们

dōu yǒudiǎnr shēngqì le
都 有点儿 生气 了。

Jiějie shuō Chūqù wán ba Chūqù wán ba Wǒ
姐姐 说："出去 玩 吧! 出去 玩 吧! 我

dōu zài jiā lǐ dàile èrshisì xiǎoshí le Shuōzhe
都 在 家 里 待了 二十四 小时 了。" 说着，

tā hái niǔ qǐle shēnzi shǒu yě bùtíng de bǎidòng
她 还 扭 起了 身子，手 也 不停 地 摆动。

Wǒ shuō Qù wǒ jiā wán xíng bùxíng Tā shuō
我 说："去 我 家 玩，行 不行？"她 说：

Bùxíng Wǒliǎ hùbǔ xiǎng ràng Zuìhòu hái shì
" 不行!"我俩 互补 想 让。 最后，还 是

姐姐 妥协 了,她 说:"算了,看 在 你 小 的 份 上 ,去 你 家 玩 吧!"

我 听了 后,高兴 极了。姐姐 比 我 大,凡事 都 让着 我。我 对 姐姐 很 感激,我 决定 以后 我们 玩 的 时候,要 好好 相处 ,好好 商量 。

[13] Discuss
English Translation

今天，我和姐姐一起在她家里玩。玩着玩着，她想去外面玩，可我却想去我家玩。

Today, my sister and I were playing at her house. As we were playing, she wanted to go outside to play, but I want to go to my home to play.

这可怎么办呢？我俩商量了半天，都坚持自己的意见。这时，我们都有点儿生气了。

What can we do about this? We discussed for half a day，and both insisted on our respective opinions. At this point, we both are a little angry.

姐姐说："出去玩吧！出去玩吧！我都在家里待了二十四小时了。"说着，她还扭起了身子，手也不停地摆动。我说："去我家玩，行不行？"她说："不行！"我俩互补想让。最后，还是姐姐妥协了，她说："算了，看在你小的份上，去你家玩吧！"

Sister said: "Go out and play! Go out and play! I've been at home for twenty-four hours." As she spoke, she twisted her body and kept swinging her hands. I said, "Go play at my house, okay?" She said, "No!" We're both civil to each other.. Finally, sister settled, she said: "Forget it, look since you are younger, we go to your house to play!"

我听了后，高兴极了。姐姐比我大，凡事都让着我。我对姐姐很感激，我决定以后我们玩的时候，要好好相处，好好商量。

I was very happy after hearing that. My sister is older than me and lets me have my way. I am very grateful to my sister. I have decided that in the future when we play, to get along with her, and have a good discussion.

Note: References to sister in this story does not mean the characters are sisters. In China, the children are accustomed to calling any girl older than them "big sister".

【14】有趣的汤米

我 有 一个 可爱的 朋友，它 名 叫 汤米，是一条 宠物 狗。

它 的 性格 很 温柔。 当 你 伸出 手 时，它 会 毫不犹豫 地 搭上 自己 的 小 爪子，和 你 握 握手 。 在 你 写 作业 时，它 会 跳 上桌 来，踩印 几 朵 小 梅花，还 高兴 地 叫 几 声 。

汤米 一 看 别人 吃 东西，就 会 跑到 别人 面前 ，站 起来，两 只 小 爪子 不停 地 拜，直到 别人 给 它 吃 东西 才 停止 。

Wǒ jiā de tāng mǐ shìbushì hěn yǒuqù

我家的汤米是不是很有趣？

[14] Tommy
English Translation

我有一个可爱的朋友，它名叫汤米，是一条宠物狗。

I have a lovely friend, and its name is Tommy, it is a pet dog.

它的性格很温柔。当你伸出手时，它会毫不犹豫地搭上自己的小爪子，和你握握手。在你写作业时，它会跳上桌来，踩印几朵小梅花，还高兴地叫几声。

Its character is very gentle. When you reach out your hands, it doesn't hesitate to hold on to you with its little paws and shake your hand. When you do your homework, it will jump on the table, make a few stamps on the table with its tiny paws, and bark a few times.

汤米一看别人吃东西，就会跑到别人面前，站起来，两只小爪子不停地拜，直到别人给它吃东西才停止。

As soon as Tommy saw someone else eating, he would run to that person, stand up, and keep pawing until they fed it.

我家的汤米是不是很有趣?

Isn't my Tommy interesting?

【15】问路

Zài yí ge zhōumò māma jiāogěi lǐ guó yì lán
在 一个 周末，妈妈 交给 李 国 一 篮

shuǐguǒ ràng tā gěi nǎinai sòngqù
水果，让 他 给 奶奶 送去。

Lǐ guó tízhe shuǐguǒ dào le mǎlù shàng hūrán
李 国 提着 水果 到了 马路 上，忽然

xiǎngqǐlai tā zhǐ zhīdao dìzhǐ què wàngle gāi zěnme
想起来 他 只 知道 地址，却 忘了 该 怎么

zǒu Zhèng fànchóu de shíhou zhíbān de lǐ yéye
走。 正 犯愁 的 时候，值班 的 李 爷爷

yíngmiàn zǒulái Lǐ guó yìbiān huī zhuóshǒu yìbiān
迎面 走来。李 国 一边 挥 着手，一边

gāoshēng hǎn Wèi cháoyáng lù yíhào zěnme zǒu
高声 喊："喂，朝阳 路一号 怎么 走!"

Lǐ yéye jiàn tā hěn méiyǒu lǐmào biàn duì tā
李 爷爷 见 他 很 没有 礼貌，便 对 他

shì'érbújiàn táizhe tóu bèizheshǒu dàbù zǒukāi le
视而不见,抬着 头，背着手，大步 走开 了。

Lǐ guó jiàn lǐ yéye bùlǐ tā dùnshí míngbai
李 国 见 李 爷爷 不理 他，顿时 明白

le Yúshì tā dàbù zhuīshàng qù Duìbuqǐ lǐ
了。 于是，他 大步 追上 去："对不起，李

爷爷，刚才 我 太 没有 礼貌 了，请 原谅 我 吧！您 能 告诉 我 朝阳 路 一号 怎么 走 吗?" 李 爷爷 听 了，笑着 说："知 错 就 改 就是 好 孩子。 我 告诉 你 吧，从 这里 一直 往前 走，第一 个 胡同 向右拐 就 到 了。""谢谢 您，再见!"

李 国 提着 水果， 蹦蹦跳跳 地 向 路口 跑去。

[15] Asking for Directions
English Translation

在一个周末，妈妈交给李国一篮水果，让他给奶奶送去。

One weekend, my mother gave Li Guo a basket of fruits and asked him to deliver it to his grandmother.

李国提着水果到了马路上，忽然想起来他只知道地址，却忘了该怎么走。正犯愁的时候，值班的李爷爷迎面走来。李国一边挥着手，一边高声喊："喂，朝阳路一号怎么走！"李爷爷见他很没有礼貌，便对他视而不见，抬着头，背着手，大步走开了。

Li Guo carrying the basket of fruits headed to the road, but he suddenly remembered that he only know the address, but forgot the directions. While he was worrying, Grandpa Li, who was on duty, came face-to-face with him. Li Guo waved his hand, and shouted: "Hey, how do I get to Chaoyang Road No. 1 ?!" Grandpa Li saw that he was very impolite, so he ignored him, folded his hand, and walked away.

李国见李爷爷不理他，顿时明白了。于是，他大步追上去："对不起，李爷爷，刚才我太没有礼貌了，请原谅我吧！您能告诉我朝阳路一号怎么走吗？"李爷爷听了，笑着说："知错就改就是好孩子。我告诉你吧，从这里一直往前走，第一个胡同向右拐就到了。""谢谢您，再见！"

Li Guo saw that Grandpa Li ignored him, he understood what happened. So, he strode to catch up: "I'm sorry, Grandpa Li, just now I was too rude, please forgive me! Could you tell me how to get to Chaoyang Road?" Grandpa Li listened, smiled and said: "Knowing you have done wrong and apologise is a good child's behaviour. I'll tell you, go straight from here, and at the first alley turn right." "Thank you, bye! "

李国提着水果，蹦蹦跳跳地向路口跑去。

Li Guo, carrying the basket of fruits, bouncing towards the intersection.

【16】半个鸡蛋壳

早上，小虫子，小蚂蚁和小蝴蝶出来玩。它们发现了半个鸡蛋壳。于是他们便找来一根小木棍儿架在上面，玩起了跷跷板的游戏。小虫子一下子把小蚂蚁顶了起来，而小蝴蝶则在一旁为小蚂蚁加油。

过了一会儿，它们玩累了。小虫子和小蚂蚁就把鸡蛋壳做成降落伞的样子。随着风，它们飞上了天空。小蝴蝶在一边为它们指引方向，带它们看到了很多美丽地风景。

到了 下午，竟然 下雨 了！它们 赶紧 降落 到 地上，躲 到 蛋壳 里，蛋壳 变成了 一个 超 极大 的 雨伞。三 个 小动物 听 着雨 点 打 在 蛋壳 上，好像 在 听着 演奏 的 乐曲 呢！

天黑 了，弯弯 的 月亮 升上了 天空 。小 虫子，小 蚂蚁 和 小 蝴蝶 躺 在 半个 蛋壳 里，望着 深蓝 的 夜空 数 星星：一颗，两 颗，三 颗。。。这时，飘 来 一 片 叶子，正好 盖 在 它们 身上，好 舒服 啊！它们 甜 甜 地 睡着 了。

[16] Half an Eggshell
English Translation

　　早上，小虫子，小蚂蚁和小蝴蝶出来玩。它们发现了半个鸡蛋壳。于是他们便找来一根小木棍儿架在上面，玩起了跷跷板的游戏。小虫子一下子把小蚂蚁顶了起来，而小蝴蝶则在一旁为小蚂蚁加油。

　　In the morning, little bug, little ant and the little butterfly came out to play. They found half an eggshell. So they look for a small wood to stick on top of it and played a seesaw game. The little bug suddenly flung the little ant up, and the little butterfly was cheering for the little ant on the side.

　　过了一会儿，它们玩累了。小虫子和小蚂蚁就把鸡蛋壳做成降落伞的样子。随着风，它们飞上了天空。小蝴蝶在一边为它们指引方向，带它们看到了很多美丽地风景。

　　After a while, they were tired of playing. The little bug and the little ant make the eggshell into a parachute. With the wind, they flew into the sky. The little butterfly guided them and took them to see a lot of beautiful scenery.

到了下午，竟然下雨了！它们赶紧降落到地上，躲到蛋壳里，蛋壳变成了一个超极大的雨伞。三个小动物听着雨点打在蛋壳上，好像在听着演奏的乐曲呢！

It rained in the afternoon! They quickly landed on the ground and hid under the eggshell, and it became a super-sized umbrella. The three small insects were listening to the raindrops bouncing off the eggshell, as if they were listening to music being played by an orchestra!

天黑了，弯弯的月亮升上了天空。小虫子，小蚂蚁和小蝴蝶躺在半个蛋壳里，望着深蓝的夜空数星星：一颗，两颗，三颗。。。这时，飘来一片叶子，正好盖在它们身上，好舒服啊！它们甜甜地睡着了。

It was dark, and the curvy moon rose up into the sky. The little bug, little ant and little butterfly were lying underneath the half eggshell, looking at the dark blue night sky to count the stars: one, two, three ... At this time, a leaf floated over and covered them, so comfortable ah! They fell asleep, sweetly.

【17】秋游

今天，我们到奉贤海湾去游玩。一路上很热闹，小朋友"叽叽喳喳"地说个不停，不一会儿就到了景点。

我们首先在老爷爷的指导下一起划龙舟。划龙舟可有趣啦，我当了一回鼓手，心情特别激动！划完龙舟后，我们来到沙地里比赛挖山芋，我一口气挖了四个呢！之后我们又去抓小鸟，抓小鱼，最后又走了一回迷宫，迷宫里面的"毒蛇""霸王龙"和"怪兽"把一些胆小的同学吓得直叫。

傍晚 的 时候，我 带着 山芋 回到

家 里，赶忙 喊："外婆，明天 您 不用 买

菜 了，快 来 看看 我 带 什么 菜 回来 了!"

[17] Autumn Tour
English Translation

今天，我们到奉贤海湾去游玩。一路上很热闹，小朋友"叽叽喳喳"地说个不停，不一会儿就到了景点。

Today, we went to Fengxian Bay to play. Our road trip was very lively, the children were talking non-stop, and we reached our destination in no time.

我们首先在老爷爷的指导下一起划龙舟。划龙舟可有趣啦，我当了一回鼓手，心情特别激动！划完龙舟后，我们来到沙地里比赛挖山芋，我一口气挖了四个呢！之后我们又去抓小鸟，抓小鱼，最后又走了一回迷宫，迷宫里面的"毒蛇""霸王龙"和"怪兽"把一些胆小的同学吓得直叫。

We first rowed a dragon boat under the guidance of our grandfather. Dragon boat can be fun, and I became the drummer, the mood is particularly exciting! After rowing the dragon boat, we went to the beach to have a dig the potato competition, and I dug four in one breath! Then we went to catch the birds, catch the small fishes, and finally walked a maze, inside the maze, there were the "venomous snake", "king dragon" and "monster", which scared some timid students.

傍晚的时候，我带着山芋回到家里，赶忙喊："外婆，明天您不用买菜了，快来看看我带什么菜回来了！"

In the evening, I came home with the potatoes, hurriedly shouted: "Grandma, you do not have to buy food tomorrow, come look at what I brought back!"

【18】好老师

上课铃响了,我飞快地向教室跑去。上楼梯时,我却不小心滑到了,膝盖被楼梯边缘蹭破了皮,鲜血直流。

我又气又急,还想往教室走。这时,以前教我们语文的李老师从这里经过,恰好看到了我。他马上停了下来,蹲下身子,非常仔细的查看我的伤口。接着,他赶忙扶着我来到医务室,一路陪着我,还安慰我说:"没事的,很快就会好的。"医生帮我涂好红药水后,她又扶着我回到了教室。

李老师这么关心我,我的心里好像被火把照亮了似的,感觉暖洋洋的。她真是一位好老师,真正的从心里关心我们,爱护我们!

[18] Good Teacher
English Translation

上课铃响了，我飞快地向教室跑去。上楼梯时，我却不小心滑到了，膝盖被楼梯边缘蹭破了皮，鲜血直流。

The class bell rang, and I quickly ran to the classroom. When I went up the stairs, I accidentally slipped, and the edge of the stairs cut my knee, and blood was flowing.

我又气又急，还想往教室走。这时，以前教我们语文的李老师从这里经过，恰好看到了我。她马上停了下来，蹲下身子，非常仔细的查看我的伤口。接着，她赶忙扶着我来到医务室，一路陪着我，还安慰我说："没事的，很快就会好的。"医生帮我涂好红药水后，她又扶着我回到了教室。

I was angry and anxious and wanted to go to the classroom. At this time, my former teacher, Miss Li, who had taught us in the language class, passed by and saw me. She stopped immediately, crouched down, and looked at my wound. Then she hurriedly helped me to the infirmary, she accompanied me all the way there, and comforted me: "It's all right; it's going to be all right soon." After the doctor applied some red colour medicine, she helped me to get back to the classroom.

李老师这么关心我，我的心里好像被火把照亮了似的，感觉暖洋洋的。她真是一位好老师，真正的从心里关心我们，爱护我们！

Miss Li cares so much about me, my heart seems to be lit up by the torch, and felt so warm. She is a good teacher, really cares about us from her heart and loves us!

【19】不倒翁

我制作的手工教不倒翁，它是用鸡蛋壳和彩纸做的。

让我来告诉你我是怎样做的吧！首先拿出一个鸡蛋，在鸡蛋的下方轻轻地戳一个洞，把鸡蛋黄倒在碗里，再用抹布轻轻的擦干鸡蛋壳。然后，轻轻地把细沙倒进蛋壳里，用彩纸做一个帽子。这时，不倒翁的主体就完成了。最后，我又给不倒翁画上眼睛，鼻子和嘴巴。

注意，可不要把不倒翁摔倒地上

啊! 摔到 地上 就 破 了, 破了 不倒翁 就
倒下 起 不 来 了。

这 就是 我 的 手工 作品, 你 也 可以
来 试试!

[19] Tilting Doll
English Translation

我制作的手工叫不倒翁，它是用鸡蛋壳和彩纸做的。

I made a tilting doll in my handicraft class. It was made with eggshell and coloured paper.

让我来告诉你我是怎样做的吧！首先拿出一个鸡蛋，在鸡蛋的下方轻轻地戳一个洞，把鸡蛋黄倒在碗里，再用抹布轻轻的擦干鸡蛋壳。然后，轻轻地把细沙倒进蛋壳里，用彩纸做一个帽子。这时，不倒翁的主体就完成了。最后，我又给不倒翁画上眼睛，鼻子和嘴巴。

Let me tell you how I made it! First, take an egg and gently poke a hole under the egg, pour out the egg yolk into a bowl, and then gently dry the eggshell with a rag. Then gently pour some fine sand into the eggshell and make a hat with the coloured paper. At this point, the main body of the tilting doll is completed. Finally, I painted the eyes, nose and mouth on the tilting doll.

注意，可不要把不倒翁摔倒地上啊！摔到地上就破了，破了不倒翁就倒下起不来了。

Be careful, don't drop the tilting doll on the ground! If it falls onto the ground, it will break. Once the tilting doll is broken, it won't swing back up again.

这就是我的手工作品，你也可以来试试！

This is my handicraft work, you can also try it!

【20】我想当一名科学家

我有一个十分美好的梦想，那就是长大以后成为一名科学家，为人类造福。。。

我想制造出各种各样的机器人，帮妈妈的饭店看门，收钱，做事，还可以给我们小朋友辅导功课。这样，家长们的工作就会减轻很多。。。

我还想培育出耐敢旱的植物，让沙漠变成绿洲，让我国北方地区不再受沙尘暴的侵袭。。。

我还要研究出各种"灵丹妙药",让人类远离疾病的困扰,让人们幸福的生活在这个美好的家园中。

不过,想要实现这个梦想,我必须要从现在开始打好基础,好好学习,否则,一切都没有办法实现!

[20] I Want to be A Scientist English Translation

我有一个十分美好的梦想，那就是长大以后成为一名科学家，为人类造福。。。

I have a perfect dream, that is, to become a scientist when I grow up, to benefit humanity. . .

我想制造出各种各样的机器人，帮妈妈的饭店看门，收钱，做事，还可以给我们小朋友辅导功课。这样，家长们的工作就会减轻很多。。。

I want to create a variety of robots, help my mother out in her restaurant, collect money and other things, and also teach us children homework. In this way, the parents' workload will be reduced tremendously. . .

我还想培育出耐敢旱的植物，让沙漠变成绿洲，让我国北方地区不再受沙尘暴的侵袭。。。

I also want to cultivate plants that are resistant to drought and sandstorm, and turn the desert into an oasis, so that the northern part of China is no longer affected by sandstorms. . .

我还要研究出各种"灵丹妙药"，让人类远离疾病的困扰，让人们幸福的生活在这个美好的家园中。

I have to invent a variety of "magic pills" to keep people away from diseases and let people live happily in this beautiful place.

不过，想要实现这个梦想，我必须要从现在开始打好基础，好好学习，否则，一切都没有办法实现！

However, to realize this dream, I must from now on, lay a good foundation by studying hard. Otherwise, there is no way to achieve my goal!

Audio Download

Link to direct download of free audio files:

https://allmusing.net/hong-meng/chinese-stories-book-3-audio/120/

OR

Scan the QR code below:

Password to download the audio files:

n%jX2tRW@4

Printed in Poland
by Amazon Fulfillment
Poland Sp. z o.o., Wrocław